MUTINY

Also by Phillip B. Williams

Thief in the Interior (2016)

MUTINY

Phillip B. Williams

PENGUIN POETS

PENGUIN BOOKS
An imprint of Penguin Random House LLC
penguinrandomhouse.com

LIBRARY OF CONGRESS CATALOGING-IN-PUBLICATION DATA
Names: Williams, Phillip B., author.
Title: Mutiny / Phillip B. Williams.
Description: [New York] : Penguin Books, [2021] | Series: Penguin poets
Identifiers: LCCN 2021008349 (print) | LCCN 2021008350 (ebook) |
ISBN 9780143136934 (paperback) | ISBN 9780525508441 (ebook)
Subjects: LCGFT: Poetry.
Classification: LCC PS3623.I5593 M88 2021 (print) |
LCC PS3623.I5593 (ebook) | DDC 811/.6—dc23
LC record available at https://lccn.loc.gov/2021008349
LC ebook record available at https://lccn.loc.gov/2021008350

Printed in the United States of America
1st Printing

Set in FCaslonTwelveITCStd
Designed by Sabrina Bowers

It's been a long time, I shouldn't have left you
Without a strong rhyme to step to
                        —*Eric B. & Rakim, "I Know You Got Soul"*

I got a lot to be mad about
                        —*Solange, "Mad"*

CONTENTS

MUTINY

FINAL FIRST POEM

In the beginning, I suspect my index is on fire.
Daystart spasmodic with hunger, my dull teeth catch
on pale figures voweling from an empty heaven. God
been left, bored too with ransom for art, allusions

stacked like reluctant saints on a pyre: Eliot, Alighieri,
Homer. The sun's glossy odyssey traces half-
moon above the horizon, clefts these alexandrine hours
into shoddy boats I'm tired of drifting toward nothing on.

"There was once a sea," I begin, having never seen a sea
nor been able to seam any time to *once*. Now, I sleep
and avoid documenting my rhyme-sourced wet dreams,
and who would collect these metered christenings?

I want to know what you must know. I own nothing
impressive. No noctuaries of gallivanting steeds, no
beloveds creeping from sun-bloodied water in a salt-
stained stolen dress, no oceans from which she stole

her voice to give to me to offer you slow-blinkingly,
awaiting "genius" and a circle of rooks (all the crows
have gone, my love, and all shovels cradling yarrow and jewels
of beetles have rusted away, revealing my face all along

held these things in unrequited climax) to crown me king.
The book is burning. Come, sit at my bedside. Let ash
fill the fugue that was your need. Now, open your hands.
Reader, read to me what you have stolen and called your life.

OF THE QUESTION OF SELF AND
HOW IT NEVER QUITE
GETS ANSWERED

In the poem, figure A is distilled to shadow and floor-looking.

Figure B musics crane-necked, anticipatory for the *nih-nig*.

I've always been a sucker for taxonomy.

The many ways I other without knowing.
I'm so Black I'm somebody's pappy lowering

his eyes to an unmarked grave. Shamecracked. Akimbo in exclusive gaze.

Lawd, Lawd, Lawd—who is I talking to and where is I? One must
prepare to be seen at all times astounded into erasure, ill-imagined.

Some of us eat watermelon in the closet, breath fermenting
and vulpine. Blessèd, to eat without being eaten.
Safe in the umbra room, dancing ensues, uncaricatured O.

Figure B sniffs figure A. Figure A is hips and textile. Puppet-pulled.
History yawns from the Os of likely weapons, a sniper in the shade.

I know because in me the dark is alive, and the dark makes plans.

FINAL POEM FOR THE WHITE STUDENTS NEXT DOOR WHO SAY "NIGGA" WHEN SINGING ALONG TO RAP SONGS LOUD ENOUGH FOR ME TO HEAR

I caught you stealing
glances of yourselves in the shrieking
mirrors of your smiles, and still

you have not found yourselves
in this self-made history bright
as a premonition. You've been

looking for your mothers
with your voices and found your names
in the pulse of Lil Wayne. I knew

already what to call you was what
you thought to call me. Please
return the *e* and *r*. You must

return to what birthed you. The nothing
rhythmlessly stomps
boot-wise over the head

of my darky sleeplessness. Last night
a young Black student screamed,
"I'm Black! I'll fuck a mother-

fucker up," trying to convince.
Nowadays, it's difficult niggering
to one's self. Just yesterday, I misplaced

3

my bottle of melatonin but said
to a friend on the phone, "I lost my melanin."
Sleepless and white, I fissured

my imagination to find in it
some semblance of you concussing
a book of speeches by MLK and chanting

"peace" in no specific direction. Responding
to my loss of melanin, my friend
screamed, "My nigga!" but I swore

he'd thrown his voice. Outside,
you cuss loudly, are angry about the beer.
Everyone needs to hear this. I raise

my blinds. I stare through the window
but can see myself as palimpsest over you all
as you stare back, approximate, catching on.

FINAL POEM AS REQUEST FOR MASKOT FOR WHITE-RAN JOURNAL, OR "THEY SURE DO LOVE THEM SOME BLACK PAIN."

Tell us duh one bout dem chirren and duh bullets dey eat

Tell us duh one bout dem roaches makin love to yo feet

Tell us duh one bout yo grandmammy's hands:
        callused and cookin, cansuh everywhere but her hands
Tell us bout her mouf too: "Oh Lawdy Jesus," "Wrench around . . . ,"
        "Bout scared me half to DEATH" she make purty sounds

Tell us duh one bout white people cuttin you
        in line [did yuh neck do that back
        and forf thing finguh waggin
        lips lippin "nuh uh no she di-int"]

Tell us duh one bout duh woman duh rope and duh bridge
        [O dere was a baby dat fell out and bumped its head
        on duh wata followin duh drinkin gourd
        or nah?]

Is you submittin to my journal or nah?
You spoken word or nah?
You hopin whitey gets his just due
        flippin duh bird or nah?

All da boys in duh hinterland killed
cause uh duh hoodie monster

You gots anymo uh dem po-lice poems wit duh
        Hippity Hop refrences wit dem thugs and da trees?
I sho love me some Hippity Hop refrences

But why thugs always smokin on dem trees
Don't dey know dey histry is
                    to run from burnin trees?

Duh way you write nigga makes me thank [of] my mama

Tell us duh one bout music comin from duh eyes
Was dat "Purple Rain" or "Duh Coluh Purple" or is it a suhprise?
Tell us "stolen milk," "watch my chirren when I'm gone,"
                    "Don't let him see me dis way," "I'm so glad Jesus is my home!"

Got anymo uh dem poems bout Celie?
Got some "Give us us free"
                    in yo packet, yo pote-folio, or yo spahklin CV?

How much fo duh WIC-EBT-lost-bus-card sonnet?
How much fo slave wenches wearin wata-melons as bonnets?

What you got up in dat verse what you got up in dat verse
                    [a couple uh guns / a couple uh blunts / a couple uh suicide
                    doors / Dior chokers / all duh shit you adore?]

Dat one gets me so hard/wet at night in duh dahk

Duh dahk got a poem too soundin jus like a knife
                    slidin through some cone-bread

Soft as a baby

Tell us duh one again bout duh baby

ORDER OF EVENTS

First, he taught us to use the dead as shawls
in the viscous winter escorting his arrival.
Next, he taught us to forget the dead
were dead, our dead, and dead because of a wager
we did not consent him to make with the thin-lipped
savior of his own pantomime. Third, he delivered
on promises that blew off the tops of homes
in places whose names he could not pronounce.
Uneasy lies the head that wears a crown
forced to fit a quiet country needing nothing
from a crown. Where once was honey unhived
competition. The drones meant for war
prepared for war. We dusted our shoulders
of Shadows' silent reconnaissance, surveilled
as practice for a massacre we did not consent to.
The royal parade pride's malady stomped
its sequence through beat drums of human skin
from which emanated a rhythm impossible
to decipher. I too would shake my ass
to the sound of stars falling night-
wise into a pit of myth-bent nomenclature
if the names sounded like home. Under eroding
circumstances, this kingdom could become home.
Under eroding circumstances, my gasp
has become home enough, love not
consented to yet detected from beneath
my mindless right hand pressing its devotion
to ritual over my heart, flag above waving heaven
and blood into the smoke-diffused sky I
quake my way through anthems beneath. Rockets
glaring off my breath forced to evidence I belong.
The crown is crooked. We straighten it
with vote-vapid hands. The crown sits too heavy
for the king to carry on his own. When it falls,
"O say can you see" strikes its inquisition.

My knees, summoned to straighten at the hinges
permission most questionably opens from,
spike the earth with a kiss. Could I
kneel my way to revolution?
Would that goad the king to unzip?

FINAL POEM FOR A KING

I used to be friends with a man who raped a woman
whom he told was too dark for anyone to believe
though he himself was no lighter than the blackhole
he had become which means he did not believe
himself thus hated himself and will hate beyond himself
though he did not know it at the time that to rape
a Black woman was to hate the world and to be dead
to want to be dead to need to be dead because to be
born from one's unfounded hatred is to be wholly
and forever zero to the white meat and she
the woman who shared her story had been for years
holding on to his violence his hatred toward her
handed off like a clue as in "What do you know
of yourself?" as in "My hatred birthed me, now so will you."

I often think of that woman, whose name
was left unshared and I wouldn't share it
even if I knew it—nor will I share his name for the law
he claims to hate for its whiteness has protected
his black revulsion, his silence an empire's
gift to its willing slave—and I wonder how much
room there is in the world for her and how much
room have others taken from her and how her story
did not stop those who heard it from, months later,
sitting in a room with her rapist, smiling, allowing,
and how the rooms of their hearts had no space
for her either, though hadn't she taken a step past
their thresholds, been invited in, not knowing
she had entered through the back door like a secret?

In undergrad, an acquaintance I had grown to love
told me her father had used the times of her mother's
absence to—

        I don't know why she trusted me
to tell me this so casually in a burger joint.
And I remember wanting her to cry
because I wanted to cry but could not cry
and why could I not cry and how else do I
show her that I hear I care I believe her and she
thanked me for listening while I sat petrified
in half-smile like a delinquent who committed
a crime and almost got away thinking more
of myself than of her as is the way of men
who want most to be the unasked-for
white knight in an already-fought war.

His childhood friend, a teenage girl
when he was six. Their older cousin, fifteen,
and they were eight. His babysitter, her saying,
"Keep this between us." Their aunt's best friend
while the aunt ran an errand: "Girl, of course
I'll watch him. He my lil husband." His neighbor
who put his hand between his legs.
His teacher whom he impregnated at fifteen.
A woman his father paid and watched as they did it—
Adults in my life have come to me as the children
they were when touched too soon and asked me
if they did something wrong. I say "no" and "therapy"
and "You didn't deserve . . ." They ask me if I'd ever
been touched too soon. I say, "I don't remember."

No woman in my family will tell me
what happened and I can't tell them
I already know had been in the other
room sometimes when it happened
heard the slaps come down heard *stop*
ring out from my _____ heard the names
heard the threats heard the quiet after
heard about the boy who pushed
my _____ off the bus about the partner
who cut my _____ across the eye the one
neighbor carefully walking up the stairs
and my _____ running to the front door
to lock it only to have to run to lock the back
door too and the knob jiggling, jiggling, ji—

If I could kill them all, God: know I would.
I'm no saint. I too have wielded a knife
to execute someone I love more than myself
because a child's rage is mercurial.
I could remember that feeling, that gilded heat.

If I could kill them all, God. Know I would
take my time. Would make a game of it. Often,
I sit daydreaming of hunting down rapists
in abandoned factories. Call me Jigsaw. I'll nod
my wooden head, a yes they never saw coming.

If I could kill them all, God, know I would.
Just call them all Isaac and I'll make them my sons.
If I could kill them all, God. Know I wouldn't
even wash my hands after. Wouldn't need permission.

When I was younger, I had a recurring dream
of an elderly man in a wheelchair tickling me
until it was not fun anymore. The dream stopped
some years into adolescence. I read somewhere
that repression leaves unlocked doors in the mind
you think are locked or merely empty rooms. Signs
that these rooms exist may never appear. I hear
nothing when I close my eyes, alone with myself,
and see the entrance into me expectantly open,
empty halls in memories where doors are blown
off hinges, rooms evacuated, torn white fabric draping
from the walls. There's a condemned house in me.

I look for him in every sun-filled room,
but every beam of light and room is him.

AND NOW UPON MY HEAD THE CROWN

In the first place—I wanted him and said so
when I had only meant to say. His eyes
opened beyond open as if such force would unlock me
to the other side where daylight gave reason
for him to re-dress.

When he put on his shirt,
after I asked him to keep it off, to keep putting off
the night's usual end, his face changed beneath
the shirt: surprise to grin, to how even the body
of another's desire can be a cloak behind which
to change one's power, to find it.

~

In the first place
he slept, he opened the tight heat of me that had been
the only haven he thought to give a name:

Is-it-mine? Why-you-running? Don't-run-from-it—as though
through questions doubt would find its way away from me,
as though telling me what to do told me who I was.

TABULA RASA

On the bus, a man sees me wearing a T-shirt of names
        of the dead. It is his seeing my T-shirt that makes the day
            glow and the inquiry in his seeing that makes it turn
        cold and pause us so that between us
he builds a morgue with his gaze, and in that morgue
        interpretation fashions itself from black cotton
            and white letters, from impatience and mercy.
        He rises to move toward me. The bus rocks
down avenues lined with playing children and liquor
        stores whose painted signs read MILK, CIGARETTES,
            WE ACCEPT WIC. When he reaches me he reaches
        for me, touches me on my shoulder until each
name listed flies from my shirt like a ribbon,
        circles my head like a marquee until each name
            stiffens from my head into compass needles
        jutting toward their unique destinations. To be circled
that way by the dead, haloed by names
        that make the bus glass shatter after each one flies
            back to the site of its owner's death.
        And I know, for I am there with each name,
have been split into eleven rays of myself to fly
        back to Los Angeles, Sanford, Oakland, Queens,
            Jacksonville, Brooklyn, Ferguson, Cleveland,
        the Bronx, Staten Island, North Charleston,
the dark bottom of the Tallahatchie River,
        each place a thread to suture the grievance
            left where the dead had been left, the names
        magnetized to a sidewalk, a door stoop,
a parking lot, a street where the bodies are not
        here, no stone rolled back but the bodies
            are gone, the names cannot bring them back
        and they shake as if mourning and I am made
to shake with them, can see the seams
        of now snapping open, the scene behind the scenes
            where vision remakes and obscures

time and place, the seams popping where
thumbs and timelines work swiftly to keep them shut.
    Somewhere behind the skull of the events,
        in the resonant nothing, I can hear it rupture
    and wonder what was there in the inconceivable
where it seems laughter pours from the dark,
    the sound of it making me afraid
        to be alone in the sepulchral streets, in the gas
    station's blinding neon, in my own body,
to return to myself with that sound as part of me
    and what then, and what now—
        a laughter like static into which the names slip,
    into where the openings have broken most
free before the eager thumbs work nimbly
    to sew it all back closed, back to the surface
        of the place where knowledge and arrogance
    wear the same mask, where a fog of faces
in their complexions of horror blanket seeing,
    and my eleven selves rush back to my twelfth self
        on that bus, reenter my body, and the man
    who touches my shoulder asks me the sources
of the names as though requesting a citation,
    but I am wearing a blank black shirt
        and tell him so, the release
    complete, his confused look his own
business as he sees the names and
    points, brushes
        his finger against me
    so that I can feel his seeing,
there, there he speaks into the wiped-clean, into
    the voided-out
        that is a blank screen onto which lives I cannot
    ever knowingly imagine
begin to begin.

FINAL POEM FOR WAR
DURING WAR

Questions for the war poem to host:
Who among us could weave one ghost
into another? Where find water hosted

but in the tulip's snapped back and tilted
cup? How count the escaped's speed by silt
dragged from one ruin to another? Wilt,

sings the sky's dayfabric unwoven into grayscale
as though night could coax from a star a paler
face, but when night arrives on the felled

back of a mule winged on either side by baskets
of water and rotten grapes, what verb is tasked
with this weight? How many missiles cast

their light above a child's gait? When do lions,
banished to the hills, water their hunger, lie on
their roars till the vultures pile on?

How many ways can I write exile
having myself never been exiled?
What is the face of exile

besides the one hidden beneath the pyre
of music peeling from a liar's
head? Bless the maenads, that they retire

only after this laughable poet is dead.

INTERLUDE: SASA AND ZAMANI

Because you were ancestor, because living dead and loved, in your necessary addiction you toed the roots of the banyan tree from underground, fiddling with your skullcap while saying my name in a mirror of groundwater. I saw you just the other day standing in the corner of my room at the corner of my eye, cornering my truth like a panther, remaining quarter-visible while I typed you into half-recollection, into forever the hand that held mine then undid the holding. Because I refuse to look the dead in the eye, I minded you like I mind dark shapes darting peripheral after I leave a room. My Egbe have hungers. My living makes room for finite cycles, a staircase spiraled to a point. If I die after my younger sister, you will become unknown, mortal-proofed. On the altar for my ancestors, I leave for you my favorite candy. You will love what I love. Florida water flares citrus from your obituary's fold. You were sweet when you were here. Forever be my father in your becoming forever.

FINAL POEM FOR AMIRI BARAKA

Crow Jane died on Baraka's watch
Must be a necromancer among us
throwing her corpseheart into a flush

of copse Autumn-bloodied nobodies
no-bodying in trellised gusts
their small dusks be-holing the view

A gestalt of crow feathers is erasure
wherever bird lands births unbirths
a leaving that is unleaving

or prison poised above the languid stupor
of bloodlake of concrete of an outline a lesson
in banality a shamemask an umbral expulsion

in catalpa drawing your daddy face
on the phone lines decomposing
a better song beneath the song

beneath the limp symbol of a blackbird's glint
hainting down the juju cauldron ripe with nails
moseying up the parted fields like Moses

in my niece's cornrows infected with caws
Crow Jane's black got a white mind that bird
never did nothing but love us like a canon

a false Nibbana blown-out Paradise Aleph in second
place lice copulate on the occipital's river imagine that
a snake stiff in a crow's beak catalectic a pendant

a luckless banner Noah's dove in reverse no never
Three-toed frog and snake fly before do the crow
Crow Jane died so Damballah could take hold

THE FLYING AFRICAN

"Kum . . . yali, kum buba tambe."

—*Virginia Hamilton*

The bird minstrels shrill vulgar
mimetics of my folklore's song.
In whispered incantations, wings scar

clean from my back, shake shadows
like pools of night over slave quarters
mangled with cotton. Belief in me

makes me a belonging, curves me
scintillant into half-moon like a scythe
cradling the sun. Anansi could never.

In Georgia, I heel-spun once
and took off toward Igboland, Atlantic
water foaming, a hellhound's maw

beneath me. Carolinian mansions undressed
to ruin as my black feathers curtained
Doric columns and draped over Ole Missus

a death veil. I wedded Cuba
and departed in a hurricane's revolving hunger,
Amadioha snatching palm leaves

from my swamp-whelmed hair. Unbreakable
tale: I shape-shift, my body many-birded, as a serpent
winds my throat, reminder of the soil that waits

against the wake of a hundred undead ships
carrying me to a living crisis. Need
by need it mattered who needed me: the enslaved

unbound by their making me. I contort
beck and call to resurrect the drowned bloating
in the dark cell of a dream. If the truth is that

the captured chose the ocean over chains,
then I am hope's raw epistle love-lettering alibis
against the grave. I carry the stolen many in my mouth,

readying for rebellion. Each captured day
I arrive with a new face carved for retribution,
my grin an orphanage of blades.

MUSHMOUF'S MAYBE-CROWN

1.

Manacled Man mangled, moreover made
menace-masked, maybe molded moribund,
mostly manipulated. Magnanimously marred,
mired mush-mouthed. Moor moored more.

Manacled Man meanly measured,
man-monkey mixed midst murky mirrors.
'Merica's Man-Man, minstrel-married
mophead, magnum man, mama's *mine*.

Mite-munched, Manacled Man mimics
martyr movements, moshes
minus music, muses: "Murder
made manifestations:

my madness my master."

2.

My madness my master.
Many mistake my mood manhandling my mode.
Maybe me making minimalist mumblings
means my matriculation—man made monster—

moves merrily, mystifying monogamy.
Mainly me mime monsters, malicing
municipalities. Me make maintainable
moans. Me menu. Me metaphor.

Me madmen's monitored mission.
Merchants masturbate
midst my mouth. Me might munch,
make men mate 'mongst my molars.

My mausoleum multiplies.

3.

My mausoleum multiplies
immemorial. Me misery, impossible
emperor, am maybe-me mid moonlight's
improvisations. Me immediate. Might's

emissary. Mayhem maims my museum.
Me improvise minutes.
Masticate memory. Mortuary
mammal. Mythic, melisma-minded,

memory makes me meet myself
minus mink, mirth, magic.
Myself's mess makes me
'member muzzle mincing mouth.

Maybe murder make my mouth mine.

4.

Maybe murder make my mouth mine.
Me embellish *mercy, mercy* midmorning.

Mourning masquerades mercy, impostor. Mercy mouths
impaled miracles. Miracles midwife my mind.

My mind implies miracles, emancipating me.
Impressive! Me embroider impeccable embellishments.

Maybe murder make my mouth mine?

Me impress embroidered emblems 'mongst my muscles.
Me emaciated emergency, am embargoed myth.

My embargoed myth emaciated imagined emergencies.
Implicated empty embraces. Emotions imitate monsters.

Emotions must make music. Me my monster, am mine,
mine, mine. Implosive, me emperor, am imprecise empire.

Maybe murder make my mouths mines.

FINAL POEM FOR THE CROW

1.

Dear Crow,

You owed an apology from the state
of poetry. We done did you a dirty disservice.

Poor thing, you must be exhausted notating
power lines with your negressive wings.

You been jigaboo and Negress, coon-
crooning ace boon koon in a slave woman's

womb. Li'l you can do, do, do. You po' Jim's
last name for the last time. Punctuating coffles,

prescribing collards while coughing up 4D hair
from church pews. Shea butter make you shine

like so? We done made you a coward in the corn, Raven n'em
cousin, a lyncher's hunched witness. Your shadow

a gate to hell and I'm 'bout to hop on through,
just to get my pen far on 'way from you!

2.

You convenient contrivance the figs feed
               their vibrant organs to, storms
in their roiling black opera munition you
                     with brieflight streaking their silhouettes, enough
               brilliance to distinguish your foes in the parallax
                       of trees, phone poles, and a child
       waiting near his tombhome for the poet
to stop killing him in the name of protest. In the name
               of Palestine, of Syria, of—too many bombs dropped
      without the country that dropped them being named.

          It's real how the poet rushes us into calamity. The poet

                  will not stop rhyming *missile* with *exile*, will always
        find another carcass and corncob crib full of limbs
             for you to deliver like a gangster. A mother dyes
her dress red and screams *blood*, screams *I am already*
               dead to repel your calamus pelting the window.
           Hexbird hoodlum, wokeface minstrel, you know
             who built the wall but only caw at the doll
       caught in the barbed wire's reaping. May we feast
           on you as you pace our eyes, foot in our mouths, a choir
               of greedy tenors with no way to escape.

FINAL POEM FOR
THE "BLACK BODY"

*"[N]o names—the lists of slaves in the book were simply identified as
'Negro man' or 'Negro woman' at the top of the ledger and
the account book followed by 'ditto' all down the page."*

—M. NourbeSe Philip*

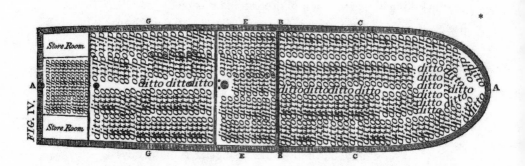

FIG. IV.

---

* I tried to love them out of their caricature, back into a name, to love a name onto them, misbelieving the rendering represented anyone but these featureless tremolos beckoning in replication a need to be held. They were not children, but their want to be wanted (their being made that way) made a thin nursery of me. How can I say no to them who have contaminated my reflection? I tried to free them, but their ink-chains, their two-dimensional silence—I found not bodies, not selves or *they*. All is "ditto" if even one is "ditto," a wild grammar taking the shape of what floats.

JANUARY 1, 2018

On Fortune.com, an article about slavery
in Libya prefaced by a Dove commercial:
"I don't want there to be white marks,"
a potential buyer says, inspecting a shirt
while a lively tune plays in the background.
The ad is for an invisible dry spray. I laugh
without meaning to as dozens of migrants'
faces interrupt the once-white screen.
Soap-white words annotate the visual: "sold
in slave markets"—but I am still
thinking of antiperspirants, about the possible
scent of an unseeable product. I am still
laughing. I remain in laughter.
It is my latest state of being, of matter.

FINAL POEM AS
TIDALECTIC ELEGY

*"The Middle Passage, rather than haunting us, is still open . . .
with water flowing forth in a constant, violent rush."*

In the wake of departure and salt spray, who looks back?
      In the wake of Atlantic afflictions, of this liminal black.
        In the wake of the taken-in, of ruptures in the track

    of a sea being entered and what entered ever-swallowed.
The wake unseals epitaphs from throats thought fallow.
    The wake spits up familiars, flesh and splinter alloy.

      The wake blamed for the neglect-fed nations
    that sculpt indifference, fluent disdain: *sunken Africans
will give AIDS to the sharks,* spoke a failed civilization.

    Dear wake, if my body is 70 percent water, how
        many likenesses have I imbibed? What shrouds
    prepare to disclose their semblances within me, bountiful

with the sweat of the thrown-overboard,
      the jumped-into-freedom, before the Lord
        could be given like a disease. Freedom bored

      with freedom's language. The necessary
revision, meaning's umbilicus severed. Dull pageantry:
    cloud shadow in the water, blackened dinghy,

      ephemera over ephemera. Legalese
of ghosts, an eroded investment, cargo seized
up in the ship's wake, a recapturing, a chronic disease,

    an annotation, sharp asterisk, perpetual annexation.
      The waves repeat their inexact canon,
    their mimetic self-mastry painting a scene

of endless transposition. What is the within?
    What is in the shipping news? The Marine
        List: *La Amistad, Aurore, Duc du Maine,*

    Trouvadore, Emanuela, Britannia (1783),
Britannia (1788), *Wanderer,* HMS *Monkey,*
    Enterprise, Alexander, Sugar Cane, Henrietta Marie,

    Othello (1781), *Othello* (1786), *Antelope,*
    Queen Anne's Revenge, Robert, Hope,
Angola, Thomas Hunter, Nightingale, the HMS *Black Joke.*

In the Mediterranean Sea over which a French warship,
    like a squall, gasps and freezes at the vista
darkening with hunger, its sailors taking pictures

of Nigerians, Ethiopians, Eritreans, Sudanese,
    as their dinghies lose their utterances in the sea.
    The Mediterranean glances at itself in migrants' eyes,

    unbalances the boat for a closer look,
while Europeans burn history from their books
    and use migrant hair to bait their hooks.

~

"I had a dream you were the ocean"

I touch each ship and hear their sons scream back, "Big Spring! Canaan!
Florence! Hazelton! Marianna! Terre Haute!" Angola both prison and not
yet, both slave ship and not yet mahogany mutilated into floatviolence.
Both nation and vulgar coloniality. Present-past self and past-present self
detect a mighty calculus in Grandma's quilt. Map to the Door of Heretofore.
Quilombos unhide from dark lines of melanated nail beds and grown pikes
that sprout buckra heads in toto. Tongues out. Ass out and weary, I
practiced marronage and ended up at Church's. Tongue out weather-vaning

grease stench toward other futures. The weather in the flowering mountains shakes like the birth of a new nachon. Ol' dude watching the gate the clouds make at the peak ain't Elegba though he sho smell like funeral flowers, a wild aunt's locked cupboard rum-wasted and doused with pennies. The likka burn like row houses on Osage, like Black Wall Street scorching wings to the backs of children, like Springfield, Illinois, charred to the fossil. O nostalgia, clamordumb muse, known silhouettes darken the water overhead. I look where one should not look in the heat of a threat. Moan-summoned, I look up.

~

"In the wake, the past that is not past reappears, always, to rupture the present"

and uses migrant hair to bait its hooks
while Europeans burn history from their books.
Unbalancing the boat for a closer look,

the Mediterranean glances at itself in migrants' eyes
as their dinghies lose their utterances in the sea
of Nigerians, Ethiopians, Eritreans, Sudanese

darkening with hunger. Sailors taking pictures
like a squall gasps and freezes at the vista.
In the Mediterranean over which a French warship,

Angola, Thomas Hunter, Nightingale, the HMS *Black Joke,*
Queen Anne's Revenge, Robert, Hope,
Othello (1781), *Othello* (1786), *Antelope,*

Enterprise, Alexander, Sugar Cane, Henrietta Marie,
Britannia (1788), *Wanderer,* HMS *Monkey,*
Trouvadore, Emanuela, Britannia (1783),

La Amistad, Aurore, Duc du Maine.
What is in the shipping news? The Marine
List as endless transposition. What is the within?

  Mimetic self-mastry paints a scene:
    the waves repeat their inexact canon,
  an annotation, sharp asterisk, perpetual annexation

up in the ship's wake, a recapturing, a chronic disease
  of ghosts, an eroded investment, cargo seized
    ephemera-over-ephemera. Legalese

  cloud shadow in the water. Blackened dinghy,
revision, meaning's umbilicus severed. Dull pageantry
  with freedom's language. The necessary

    could be given like a disease. Freedom bored
  into the jumped-into-freedom before the Lord,
with the sweat of the thrown-overboard,

  prepared to disclose their semblances within me, bountiful.
    Many likenesses I have imbibed. What shrouds,
  dear Wake, if my body is 70 percent water. *How*

will I give AIDS to the sharks? Speak, failed civilization.
  Sculpt indifference, fluent disdain. Sunken Africans
    the Wake blamed for the neglect-fed nations.

  The Wake spits up familiars, flesh and splinter alloy.
The Wake unseals epitaphs from throats thought fallow.
  Of a sea being entered and what entered ever-swallowed—

  in the wake of the taken-in, of ruptures in the track;
  in the wake of Atlantic afflictions, of this liminal black;
in the wake of departure and salt spray—who looks back?

HERALD

His back arched as though through his heart
his shoulder blades would push into the air
their ante-wing. I have seen such doves go
into what seemed like light but was another
cave. What feathers weight a cage over my heart?
But, Cassandra, no one asked you. The goring that
sudden entry into any sanctuary could become
was not me alighting. "What love?" was
the question from the mouth his back and the bed made.

THE FIELD

The battered field is hateful without remorse,
is as seductive as what is familiar: a wild horse
who long ceased being horse, had become beauty itself

failing as the field has failed or someone has failed
the field with overuse, the gray soil too sparse,
its blond grass in tight nubs and stiff as scimitars

that jut from the earth as declarations of war.
The barrenness cannot feed the hares who feed
the foxes who feed the bloodlust of men.

There is a leafless dogwood stunted
in its naked reach. A storm rolls over
the jagged boughs raking the black air's

softened belly until lightning clarifies its scars.
Scimitars could scar a belly with their sharpness,
with their curves like a gleaming succubus

sliding on each nerve's nylon until the harp is
undone. Or the harp is played to the tune
wind makes undressing an arid field. This is love

if someone says so. A man weeps
to soft music in his house though nothing
can hear him outside his window, his cry

a ripple in a pond after a frog leaps out
then leaps back in, a word spoken
by mistake that the speaker wants to take back.

The word could be like love too if broken,
more broken than the shrill gate outside
swinging open then shut, obliterating entrance

and exit. Here waits the god whose flute reveals and hides
the way. She is mischievous with her song
coming off the rusted hinges. The gate is edged

by two stone pillars, both topped with pots
once holding lavender, now holding moldy soil,
one sweet smell deposed by another. Rot

and the bones left bare is the story of the hare and fox
while the felled horse crafts the field's ugliness.
Its wraith hooves crush the ground. Let the gate

squeal shut against that bestiary. The world's
revision of itself roils through the sky. Storm
of bruised clouds, lightning and the last living beast

revealed in bursts: first its outline. Next its distant
maw made clear in that moment of light. Then two
cobalt eyes, an abacus by which to count the days.

HUNTER

When you were mine though not
mine at all permanently, just a body
for loneliness, a loneliness interrupted,
interruptive—

        the sky opened like a secret in a mouth

mouth with a word in it

word with an arrowhead in its flank: Love, small

creature it was

          crying in the night beneath me

FINAL POEM FOR THE DEER

Deer asleep on the side of the road. No, deer
dead there as always, preserved in the Book
of Symbols. Deer with its flies and uncanny
arrows in its sides like compass needles, or
fleshless wings. Deer whose hooves puncture names
in the snow. Deer who knows your name.
Deer a white-tailed gnostic in the woods.
Deer you get lost in. Deer with a ribbon
of brass bells around its neck and an iron
sword in its antlers' altar. Deer emperor
surveying a funeral from afar, hoofing open
cracks in the vagaries of the fool
who wanted a dear. Deer in the mind taking
place of the dear, always its assignment. Here,
the casket carrying the father is a deer,
four cloven hooves upon the red carpet, a blown-up
photograph of the father's past face a road
sign saying "The future is still."
Boy who refuses to view his body's father.
Afraid of the face he will not recognize,
for addiction has its way with flesh. Deer
casket marching out the church to where
the earth is gentler to flesh, strips it patiently.
Deer carrying the dead in its spine cradle.
The scent of pears beckons from the basinet
of bone. The dead carrying the dead. The arrows
in the deer tremble toward their cardinal affairs:
the skin someone forgot the feel of, the mama
who never said goodbye, the daddy whose belly
rolled on its side like a truck-crushed deer.
There is no daddy here. The father sits up
in his casket, startled, his funeral full
of his sons, no, his one son repeating
like a paper cutout. A forest of sons
in which the deer tilts its decorous head
into the father's grave and sips.

FINAL POEM AS NOCTURNE
INTO AUBADE, OR SONRISE

I do not find Osun in somebody's son I sonned
while his gold fronts flashed a summer dress
in the back of me bucking to be
ridden by his tongue like his Virginian drawl
was first to get down my draws like that like that.

Not everything masculine is mine, but I make him
mine for modernity. Sixty-watt bulb spun
mosaic by ceiling fan and
this bed creaks like a church pew and
it was Sunday when he came so he my Sunday Man,

though I prefer Thursday Man's selflessness:
before returning to his lover, he balances sunlight
on his tongue tip. He parts my legs to gift.
My hairiest part yawns like a waking bear.

FINAL POEM FOR THE BIOGRAPHY OF A BLACK MAN AS ANIMAL AND HIS ENFORCED EMBRACE OF A HUMAN PRAXIS

Slaughter lurks in the afterpasture. Perhaps
Being being blurred in the legible demands self-
captivity: his tail whipped mind-wise

tight circles of animus, or draped, equine. Flies
decorate the wake of his imagined stampede.

He was just walking, sweetie. Chewing gum,
not hay. It is exhausting to explain his non-horns
tearing through the thin gauze of civilization:

what is believed to be true must convince. Faith,
then, a requisite text, as the Lamb is to God?

Though bipedal and asthmatic, he was made centaur,
synching briefly humanity to his half-life; it made sense
where he stood that he stood on fours when sad,

like a chair carved Trojan, carted into his life,
that he could neither sit in nor shake colonizers from.

His human half shivered pronouncements
while his buck bottom flattened the field;
the meniscus of the meeting halves ahiss

with hair smooth as clay and skin
the same color, dull as a shy twin.

Brusquely present, the centaur's precise measurements—
snout to kitchen where a blade-sharp fade sunsetted—
were bestiaried palpable, flanking love-letter

marginalia for his dick stretched by bewildering estimates
and inquiries about his fondness for trees and bones.

There was a poet in him cadavered
by liturgy: *I am, I am, I am* his ruptured
correspondence, his bewitched ontology

he could no more stamp out than stomp
clear its fire-fucked flag of himself.

He grows tired of proving his humanness without
his permission, for the language won't cohere
to his nature, won't make praying away the hooves

in the minds of others secede from his neigh
of perfect speech. He heeds neither indecency.

The beast squats on his chest
and the human writes its full-
of-itself self into full self in a form

he is rack-pulled into or trough-bent grandly over,
while moralists taxonomize his grandmas' pleasure.

"The ancestors died for—" but the living
talk over the dead to protect their sons,
thinking the chains' clink a ghost leash,

but the man knows no dogs span these thrones
neither whip nor Bible could dismantle.

The centaur is dead and so is its maker.
The man removes his clothes and feels.
He does not want to be paw or possible.

He wants to be alone, private, not your agreement.
He wants impossible. Unlearnèd without reign.

BLACK JOY

"I would like to help someone to live after my death"

—*written on a donor card*

That collective moan
in Greater White Stone Church
had a body to it that I saw
as a child and mistook
for love itself, built from the silk
of sobs in the sanctuary.
The moan a language that is said to
confuse the Devil out of knowing
your business was itself a confusion
of visions, the coming into being
of liminality itself for neither joy
nor solace triumphed in the relent-
less catechisms, the wails
that were pure pain tossed up
to the ceiling or rocked from the gut
to the floor. "Lay your burdens down,"
said the pastor but they would not
stay down. Every Sunday, hymnals
sopped up sorrow after sorrow
that had no navigable ending.
Every Sunday, my grandmother
called upstairs to my mother
to see if we were going to service
with her, and we did, and I saw
the mostly elderly congregation
greet her as "Sister Williams"—and
I remember how, when I was a teenager, church
no longer a pastime, my grandmother
died and no one who loved Jesus
came to send her on her way to Him
or visit her in her living illness. Limbo,

purgatory, the church the gateway to
nonexistence, a holding cell for the deceased,
the wanting to die. That you can be clean
does not mean you can be made clean.

Saint Liminal visited last night
in their fog body that smelled of perfumes
and back of the throat, frozen birds
that paraded atop women's heads
and funk in a neck dip's decanter.
I asked, "What happened to joy?"
It had been many mornings. It was
supposed to come then. Saint Liminal
tilted their head to their shoulder and spoke
from their ear in the voice of three octaves
striking the air at once. They said, "Hennessy
drips from the poplars this crucial
conflict this hay in the middle
of the harm feeding the beast in this burning
barn in the naysayers veins this history
dripping in the Hennessy this blunt
incantation leathering thick black lips
this shoe-shine grin this
If you grin I'll let you live this
I'm alive and I'm enough half-
lie this loving and living
off the dead this happiness in spite
of this happiness in spite this
mistake that you sing because
you happy and because you free and not
because grief has a song
this wingless sparrow
for an eyeless god this singing
when Tim survived Chicago but was shot
in Cali somewhere this singing and he still

dead these Black scholars demanding joy
laughing to the bank with stolid books
written with an inflexible air of moralistic angst
with hands that push out push away the Tims
and Tim's body the only prelude you know
this activist laughing face-smashed
on concrete on a police car's hood
and the cops laughing and they laughing
together this noose in a history
museum stunned in its headless gasp
this noose on your head you call
your burden your inheritance your nuance
you using Emmett Till like a mirror a muse
wearing his gin fan like a Pulitzer
this noose on the doorknob
your reflection convex in the past tense
shine they call you and you do
you grin you show your still-yours teeth
those souvenirs in the dusk
those stones marking an ever-living grave."

And Saint Liminal straightened their head
and touched that once-talking ear
to their shoulder and spoke in rain playing
a drum, "I am the archangel draped
in pigeon feathers. I read insignias
carved into your pathos. I translate
sand sifting from top to bottom. I arrange
stars in man's imagination to constellate
prisons for gods and maps
to an ordinary freedom. I speak
all the world's languages lost and here
and yet to come. But when you ask
of joy's arrival I see nothing
but a line bisecting stone and no water

leaks forth. Nothing but a wooden dog
pierced in its back with nails. I see joy
erasing the one who seeks
to be modified by it. I see the legible
scratched illegible by an always-
forthcoming validation. Joy come
in the morning. It is here
an eternal night." When they left,
the sun had come up but joy
was still absent, which meant the sun
was not real. I grabbed a stone
and threw it at the sky.

JUDGMENT

I stand where I would have been covered
in falling blood—the point of the pierced
body—my reflection in the bronze skin
of Christ sculpted into crucifixion, hanging as if just
put into history, His brown head at the nadir
of its nod as if the very floor had summoned Him
to look, He eternally forced into this position
that both casually welcomes and warns,
neither of which I wanted, which makes it
difficult to look, so I stare, instead,
at the marble floor's swirl of frost
and liquid bone, of tempestuous fog,
swirling the way I imagine
squalls inside the body, squalls shape-
shifting like a story passed
between lips where the flesh is
soft and the story's plot—as twisted
as the chimera with its lion's head,
its snake's tail, its goat's body, a thing
to fear, to worship, to sacrifice—the plot
billows like smoke from the bronze
stomach of the Sicilian bull
where three human skulls were removed;
I name them *Perilous*, *Dictum*,
and a name I will not share
with you, no, but I will share that sage
and frankincense breathed out
from beneath burnt bodies was like a name
to a kingdom of appetite and sweetness spoken,
charred skin raised like hands eager to claim
the naked bodies dancing around it,
their sweat seasoning the air, this the story
told to me: screams crawled through a pipe
into an emperor's chamber, spurious
music, bones of the roasted victims shone

brilliantly once the bull's belly-door opened,
opal, pearl, the many things a body can
become, skeletal towers, well-chiseled
testimonies woven into necklaces,
an adornment warm as touch.

FINAL POEM FOR
THE FAMOUS POET

Woundwondered, they circle

you: headless monument erosion had—
before they thought they knew you though did not—
claimed.

Thick fog hides shoulder-up your unhead, hides
your excellent circumscribed height beneath
which, chanting, unaware,
they wreath your senseless marble feet.

They loudwrath where loud finds no place to enter
you and enter their own unthought: rage-
bright beacon to nowhere
that had they unfollowed, had they retraced their steps
away from their own unimagining—?

      Ozone settles your barren shoulders that are more
like than unlike their our-mouths-open-our-heads-mourning-
ourselves selves.

JANUARY 28, 1918

Porvenir, Texas

Myth: In the Book of America, the desert cracked open once
the inquisitors coveted the questioned's land. Livestock
fell diseased when the clamorous mob appeared
at the townspeople's doors. Night-woven wings eclipsed
logic. That the mob visited twice, both times
unblinking stars measle-ing the sky, both times "prisoners"
taken. After the first taking, the "prisoners" returned.
After the second, torn from the Book of America,
the mob killed fifteen men and boys. And the irrigated water
from the Rio Grande leapt up, rejected the bloodied earth.
The crops dropped to the ground and crawled into
a decaying sleep. One hundred forty survivors packed their eggs and books
and escaped to Mexico. When they crossed the river, they turned
into hues of blue, the sound of an owl unspooling its prey.

Eutimio Gonzales (37), Longino Flores (44), Alberto García (35)

To poeticize could be and often is interpreted as "to make beautiful."

What is the border between tragedy and beauty?

The tragedy is the Porvenir Massacre of 1918.

What now of beauty?

To poeticize could mean to view more deeply and invest in the risk of what is found,
as in "to speculate."

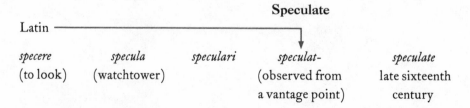

Speculate

Latin				
specere	*specula*	*speculari*	*speculat-*	*speculate*
(to look)	(watchtower)		(observed from a vantage point)	late sixteenth century

Spectacle

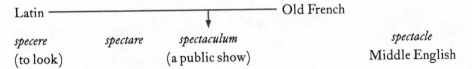

Latin ———————————————————— Old French

specere   *spectare*   *spectaculum*   *spectacle*

(to look)   (a public show)   Middle English

To make, from one's sight, a performance of what has been seen or a re-creation of
the act of seeing.

Where *to see* means "to imagine." To write truth or write torture?

With generosity or with a torch lit under history's feet?

One could be speculative, as in:

        The cavalry's horses bow in the afterbirth

      of clamor, blood in their hoofprints' bowls,

    blood imitating bush shade and widow skirt, blood

  veining desert sand down the spiral staircase

of its seeping. And who descends the decline, soft grave,

footprints breeze-wiped from the map? Blood

  in the mesquite, pyrrhuloxia singing bloodsong bush

    to bush, a red flock burning the bush. Let God speak

      of bullets painted fifteen shades of red and elders

        taking turns returning their sleep to hollow houses

          housing wind in their windowless skulls—

but in service to whom or what? A hoof

of the beast of beauty imprinted on the page,

but beauty's hide hides the history.

Viviano Herrera (23), Pedro Jiménez (25), Serapio Jiménez (25)

Fiction: Fifteen men and boys of Mexican descent visited me in a dream on the anniversary of their murders.

Fact: Avoiding the constant onslaught of media concerned with a presidential candidate incapable of correctly pronouncing *Iran*, I made my way to Instagram in search of solace and found, instead, a photograph on the Zinn Education Project of Longino Flores, a resident of Porvenir and victim of the massacre. In the photo, he is surrounded by family.

I wondered why I'd never learned about this massacre, this (I called under my breath) lynching (as though to call it so were mere speculation and not fact). Of course, my not knowing was the point of the mass killing and leveling of the town. Leave no evidence, no trace, and in that absence, anything can be drawn. A gun. A pretty metaphor.

The Book of America is one of secrets inasmuch as shame of one's heritage in hatred makes ineffectual any attempts at reconciliation between the past and the present.

"Why can't we just leave the past in the past?"

But in service to whom? Or what?

In the photograph shared by Arlinda Valencia, her great-grandfather, Longino Flores, is arced by women, one of whom is her grandmother, Juana Bonilla, and children. He sits beside another relative, Rosendo Mesa, who is Valencia's grandfather. Their ranges of brown exhaust the monochrome.

Macedonio Huertas (30), Tiburcio Jaques (50), Ambrosio Hernández (21)

The *Advanced English Dictionary* defines the noun usage of *frontier* as

1. "a wilderness at the edge of a settled area of a country"
2. "an international boundary or the area (often fortified) immediately inside the boundary"
3. "an undeveloped field of study; a topic inviting research and development"

> That borderlands have also been called "frontiers."
> That some believe there is a crossable border between
>   human and savage that should not be crossed.
> That some believe they are the sole "human" who could
>   never become something less.
> That some believe "human" is our ontological apex.
> That the "savage" finds its shape in the mind of
>   the "human."
> That the Texas Rangers, U.S. Cavalry, and four ranchers
>   shot those fifteen men and boys in the "wilderness."
> That the wildest field is the imperial imagination.
> That Captain Fox called the fifteen men and boys
>   "bandits" on their own land.
> That the bodies of the killed were discovered by Henry
>   Warren, an Anglo-American schoolteacher, and his
>   student, Juan Flores (13), son of Longino Flores.
> That a son had to find his father's corpse that way.
> That anyone must find a corpse and relate to it against the
>   routine of living, against memory.
> That the remaining residents of Porvenir returned to
>   Porvenir and brought their dead back with them to
>   Mexico for burial.
> That the dead had to cross two borders: living to dead,
>   home to exile.
> That this is the seal and perfection of exile: revision.
> That the U.S. Army razed the town of Porvenir,
>   which translates in English to "future."

Manuel Moralez (47), Román Nieves (48), Pedro Herrera (25)

What is the Anglo-American wilderness if not an abomination of the mind, an
    exaltation of the mind's tumult?

In what organ does the never-seeing of brown faces begin?

How to incorporealize another with such ease, citizenship made invalid by a want?

Extralegal: a feral Anglo amendment.

What do we call the frontier of the unexplored wilderness that was the Texas
    Rangers' ferality?

What Anglo deed for the deed to the land?

What do we make of the fifteen killed being both shot and stabbed?

What was summoned during that rite, magic slapping the ass of massacre?

We are captivated by the possibility of a freedom impossible to receive from the
    ones who promised it.

Antonio Castanedo (72), Severiano Herrera (15), Juan Jiménez (16)

Myth: The 140 survivors of the massacre did not need
to carry back the dead from where they were left dead.
When they abandoned Porvenir for refuge, the dead stood
like Christ, fingered each other's wounds, and the wind
said, *Yes, this is banishment where once was flesh.* They walked
in the country of their families' shadows as they crossed
the Rio Grande into Chihuahua. They hitched
their feet to a raft of air and glided across the water behind
their loved ones, who, when the youngest one turned,
all turned and saw the fifteen men and boys wedded

to their 140 umbras darkening the future behind
their leaving. When asked if the fifteen were alive or dead,
the wind said, *They are home. They are in your hands.*

FINAL POEM FOR THE BULLET

When the bullets overhead ricocheted
off the metal fence and junk cars grave-
stoning the junkyard, and when my uncle

shouted for me and my friend to duck
beneath the torrent of lead zip-lining
the air from an unseen source,

and when screams scratched throats keenly
till echoing the bullet din approaching no target
with aim or intention precise enough to reach

anyone but the innocent, and when my legs
refused to unfold from beneath me to follow
friend and uncle through the gangway

of a neighbor's house until being alone
was more frightening than hot shells
finding all the ways to smolder through, and when

my brutal desire to live led me to safety
acquired in an alley where rat corpses perfumed
away gun smoke of which I'd grown nostalgic,

and when laughter broke from our lungs
as if surviving didn't mean tomorrow's fury
could second-chance us toward alternative deaths,

and when I look back within myself at the pleasure
fear made possible, and when my ten-year-old breeziness
degraded to *damn, we alive* and the piss-sprayed,

Colt .45, crackpipe-laden alley corroborated
echoes of my voice in the climate of what tried
to kill us—the weather itself cracking its neck

into thunder until an hour's dismantling
manifested a system of continuous reckoning
with the possibilities of every broken bottle

mirroring my prostration's erotics. And if when
I think back to that alley leading to an empty
lot where a house of addictions once laughed

from glassless windows, if I render this re-
memory to reclaim that bullet-lost child, and if
I find him glistening like a just-born species,

wearing the eyes of my mother and the lips
of my father, holding a sword in one hand
and a scale in the other, counting backward

from ten, as when in the hollow of a nightmare
the nightmare's attendee suspects zero's nothing
brings back the world the nightmare fed from,

as if at the end of the end was a lesson,
as if at the end of the end was a form?

"NE ME QUITTE PAS":
I PUT A SPELL ON YOU:
NINA SIMONE: 1965

A single pant leg dangles from the chair.
Mud from the hem leaves graves on the floor.

Collapsing star: the last button
      of your shirt caught
            between my teeth.

Cricket: a record player cracks
                  its skipping obsessions.

A single pant leg dangles from the chair.

Stars: dust from your ankles glides up
slats of street light.

      Où l'amour sera roi: only the pits
          behind bent knees are kingdom.

Mud from the hem leaves graves on the floor.

Your underarm holds a nest of burnt leaves
I rub my face against. I smolder in the key of animal.

A single pant leg dangles from the chair,

a cougar unrolling the cologne
of a doe from its tongue.

      Où l'amour sera loi: my bare feet run
         against the headboard.

Mud from the hem leaves graves on the floor.
A single pant leg dangles from the chair.

FINAL POEM FOR THE MOON

My first lover, my clavicle's chiseler
sculpting me into blue lamentation

and crucible for your lunacy,
summon me to scuttle forward—

cancer moon, cancer rising—and fill
myself on your dust-flashed milk,

your gray honey black-green grasses
use to sharpen their nightblades. My paramour

who gowns me in a yawning glint, Helios's
canvas by which you find your aspects,

find your shape misshapen in seven-eighths,
your eighth self finally filled with ochre blood

or the ruddy salutations of familiar fever.
You pass your sickness to me like fervor,

my heart a moon learning all its phases
at once. My idiolect and diaphragm,

deliberate disc slipped from Thoth's spine,
Elysium I pitch my body beneath, white morning

glories opening from my sweat-flushed back.
I feel my veins harp-pluck toward you. I rise

like any body of water compelled into risk,
pulled up the god-ladder of your gibbous.

You perfect your appetite in my blood,
hematite of harvest, scolecite that pulls

my bloodwaves to zenith in your skull
of good omen, your lambent weight

witness to worship and worry. I, a sun-celibate
celebrant ensconced in pearl. My mood unravels

in your fingerless hand. I dance lute-backed
in the armory of your niveous eye. Your snake-fang

posture I hang from my ear, your crescent
weaning me off your nectar. I will grieve

your circumference, your diameter, your secant
and chord as you renew yourself with erasure:

Moon as a mouth no more.
Moon as a wound no more.
Moon wound round my fists
no more. Moon in the grips
of hunger, moon chip-toothed,
goat-eye round in shock no more.
Moon no beast aspires to kiss.
Moon the color of my coming
no more. Misery moon. Moon
dipped in a wail. Moonsick
no more. Moonward, dust floats
but lingers no more. Moon-heavy
chimney, no more. Moon-washed
tongue washing me, no more. Full
moon night's chandelier no more.
How high the no-more moon?
The cow jumps over the nevermoon.
Moon River no more. Wider than a mile,
my arms take the shape of you no more.
Do not watch me while I look for you,

in the galaxy that breathes your many names:
Tsukuyomi, Coyolxāuhqui, Chang'e, Khonsu.
I am malaised by moonglut, moonstruck,
lunatic eclipsed by my lips' supplicant O!

THE VOID

Our dog died in the ugly disaster
that is aloneness. She died on
the first floor, in my sister's apartment,
on a makeshift pad shifted halfway

out from under her. And I caught the center
of her dying, the shake, the after-bit
tongue swelling from her maw.
My girl. Good girl. She half-died alone

and finished with us there.
My sister and I rubbed her side
and she shook and blinked then blinked
no more but breathed a slow breath

as I rubbed her head then kissed her
forehead. Even in death she was mine
to kiss. She was not ugly. Much like
the story of the boy from school

who was shot in the head and lived to talk
about it and lived to hear us all talk about it,
the hole that needed the help of others
to close. And his neighbors around him looked

into the hole in his head as if slowly realizing
they'd all that time been unburying themselves. And I
imagine the hole like a howl from a dog,
like the diamonds in a chain-link fence

that let sight in but not the flesh. This
is the end, do not enter or take part in
what little you've been allowed to see.
Howl like a warning. Howl like a plea.

Do not pass. Do not step into this shape
in which everything ever missing takes shape:
the dead dog buried in the backyard,
the contour of sorrow that is any boy's back

darkening then disappearing altogether
from the door on his way to school,
on his way back
but he must leave first. Everything

must leave before it comes back.
Even the trees
lining the one-way streets flanked
by liquor stores bright as the mansions

of devils. Even the trees must first catch fire,
drop their fire, stand naked in penance
as we rake their burnt garments to the gutter.
Yes, even wakefulness must go toward sleep

and sleep must wake. Even the body
leaves then returns
as dirt, as a mind reeling into itself,
a brittle recollection:

Was our dog thirteen or fourteen when she died?
When I kissed her forehead, was she
already gone or still passing through,
the last bit of her dying mixing

with my sister's breath, the vet appointment
of no use now. I closed her eyes. *It's no use*, howls
the entrance wound but they fixed up the boy
who spoke another language for a short time,

the trees bowing to hear him better
beyond their dancing boughs, in spite
of their leaves that let in a little mothlight,
a little streetlight so that gaps of leaf-

shaped darkness gasped across his face,
mouth-shaped leaves on his face,
and they spoke back to the hole, *We too leave.*
We all leave. Hush. You'll come back. Lazarus.

Concrete Christ. A memory.
A haunting. A possession
like an illness, like a bullet,
like a dog's eyes staring back

then merely open
with no looking involved,
like a boy's head
babbling on.

FINAL POEM FOR
MY FATHER MISNAMED
IN MY MOUTH

Sunlight still holds you and gives
your shapelessness to every room.
By noon, the kitchen catches your hands,
misshapen sunrays. The windows
have your eyes. Taken from me,
your body. I reorder my life with
absence. You are everywhere now
where once I could not find you
even in your own body. Death means
everything has become
possible. I've been told I have
your ways, your laughter haunts my mother
from my throat. Everything
is possible. Fatherlight
washes over the kitchen floor.
I try to hold a bit of kindness
for the dead and make of memory
a sponge to wash your corpse.
Your name is not *addict* or *sir.*
This is not a dream: you died
and were buried three times. Once,
after my birth. Again, against
your hellos shedding into closing doors,
your face a mask I placed over my face.
The final time, you beneath my feet. Was I
buried with you then? I will not call
what you had left anything
other than *gone* and *sweet perhaps*. I am
not your junior, but I fell in love
with being your son. Now what? Possibility
was a bird I once knew. It had one wing.

FINAL POEM FOR THE
"FIELD OF POETRY"

In the grip of a nor'easter,
you come bearing grief,
have in pieces not come
in peace. You arrive bladed
with certainty. You slam shut
the car door and smolder
before the locked cabin, rough
trip up the Hudson as you distracted
yourself with a list of flowers awaiting
deft penmanship to groom them
tight and blow them clean.
News of your brother's death
intercepted your drive to this
residency, fellowship
among the crude Madonnas
of empty mailboxes draped in robes
of days-old ice. You have not written
about the passing of family
before, their antagonistic absences.
Intrusive their teething
tombstones in the brain. Pill
after pill to sleep, to create,
to erase, you swallow and scratch
into a notepad what the frozen earth
refuses: bougainvillea, lilac, burning
bush. Another close kin added
to the Bible's kept obituaries.
You hated your brother's left
eye, unruly wanderer settling
away from you and observing
a world you could not sense. Glossy ivy
in all its tenure, the tender fingers
of buckeye. The white page

frozen before you like rime. You
dig and discover what you already knew:
decaying kin, meandering roots
catching his beautiful ankles. You
were looking for a way out through
beauty but beauty only goes
where needed. On the pad you write: *enough*—
what you've had, how much
more of you there is, how
much of you will be left when you're gone.

THE ASPHODEL

Yes, afterlife, but also flower,
though not its color, rather the star-
break from the pinnacle,

pointing in all directions.
A kind of greed, a kind
of giving up of one's self.

But not retreat. Offering.
But not with fear. Love,
if love can make of a self

a reaching that does not end.
He had come back to him after
much time had passed.

It was the living-past
and it wasn't. It was
the fully blossomed Xs

bending beneath him
who was thought dead:
get the hell out my life,

though he returned. Shield-
less. A field of sky
breaking, breaking. A door

knocked on, a door
like a voice
opening.

SHAME

It begins with a memory of feet and above
the swollen ankles of Grandma Elizabeth's leg
cartographic with varicose veins bulbous

and slurring beneath my fingertips as I traced
what I thought was the blue of sorrow lacing
its way like an endless brook through her body

which was a body whose toes I had rubbed one
at a time with lotion to the sound of her
chewing on a peppermint or breathing slow

and hard as I relieved whatever journey
from beneath her feet sour with duty
and the power to make a walk from room to room

into a meal and game of checkers where I learned
that stacking two soldiers made a king
which would become useful later in life

as I found myself building lonesome towers with my body
and another's while we catalogued our grievances
with the sharing of tongues and here one desire

usurps another but I'll mend this memory
toward honesty for my grandmother's feet
knew speed and precision when necessary

to run across the squeaking floor for a broom
to whack the shit out of me if I frightened her
while she exited the bathroom pausing

right as she turned off the bathroom light and let
her fingers linger on the knob just a bit
as though anticipating the boy me's hunger

to hear her scream with a round soprano
Stupid! You trying to kill me? And here again
the truth stalls because beneath me

on the first floor where her room was a kingdom
of perfumes shawls and jewelry this woman
up and died while I lay in bed on the second floor

right above her and I was sure the chill
I felt was either her passing through the floor
and through me then through the roof

and into the sky where the morning sun was still
cool and from which chickadees dropped their small bodies
into the grass for seeds to pulverize in trees

or it was the angel of my thinking
unblanketing from me my own innocence
knowing that my old lady went

somewhere and left her body behind
to be found by her children and for a moment
I was closest to her just a single story away

meaning the narrative that was the air itself
crawling between my floorboards and her ceiling
was the last thing we shared and no one else

can have that and here the dark bathroom
and the metal doorknob with her fingers placed
on the chilly arc in the darkness is how she

slowly unlocked me from myself like the sun
unlocked from my body its own shadow
and I hated myself for being so unwilling

to let death do what death does and witness
the final days of her hardly sipping water
her lying in bed alone and endlessly tired

and my selfish teenage self is here now
looking up from the cloud of this memory
shaking his head and swearing under his breath

swearing at me even now too shy or too absurd
with shame to run from that old house and into
the distraction of maple tree seeds whirligigging

their papery blades into the weeds and the white
fluff of dandelions and into the street
and scream something about it being too much

or not knowing how to love then so *lay the fuck
off me man just lay the fuck off* so I must forgive
him who is my earlier self his avoiding that room

his avoiding her eyes yellowed by chemo
his avoiding her feet and his now missing
that cane tapping out the minutes of the day

that now his later self holds in the highest regard
as I lie alone to sleep listening to my downstairs
neighbors make love in their softest voices.

FINAL POEM FOR GRANDMA
ELIZABETH'S CANCER

Can I have this dance, White Light, you old worn
and loose-lip gossip? You say it's time.
No. My grandson has to rub my feet first.
Can't break tradition for a little Death
eager to get on with his business. Give
respect to the ones you take. Be patient

'cause I ain't rushing. I've been a patient
and bed-rested to tears. Hiding these worms
nobody call hair no more. Can you give
Constance, my daughter, a dream? Warn her time's
eating itself to the bone to stall death.
Rest awhile with me, Old Light. I'll go first

call of the sparrow tomorrow morn. First
answer me this. Am I cute? Greg was patient
netting this wig on his mama's bald death.
Can't look all that bad. Spent hours warring
eagerly with what's left of my hair. Time
rocked in that corner, quiet. What you give?

Could you rub my cold, stiff feet for me? Give
a final shock to my toes. Veins left first,
nook-and-crannied into varicose. Thyme,
chamomile, and spearmint oil patiently
eased on each heel. Rub it in, now. Yes. Worm
right in that spot with your bony thumb. Death,

can I marry you where I'm going? Death-
afraid, my last man had nothing to give.
Not like you, swooping up in here a worn
cyclone all flame-eyed and torn tendon. First
evening a godly man visit, patient.
Rummage in my closet for a shawl. Time

come that I get ready for our date, timed
almost perfectly. I've been so lonely, Death;
nurturing shadows with my breasts. Patience
can wear thin and I hear frail wings giving
early morning their hollow-boned song. First
razor of sun come cutting up my worn,

bloated legs. Patience: I've had it to give.
Yes, now it's time to shed this skin's long death:
empty bedpans, first light breeze. Child, this warmth.

FINAL POEM OF PERSONA

Who summoned me? Who thinks my gaze
is a wheel of thread to sew wings onto backs
that never had wings? Who traced the maze
sunset makes on the water to lead me back?
The air is caustic here and rotten milk
spills from the flowerbeds. The earth is iron-
stenched. There is blood like unwound silk
ribboning from a body. Whose child has learned
their history? Who's found the door but can't get out?
Whose words do I perform from my sealed mouth?

MASTERY

The masters are yet dead. Wanting to be human,
I tried to rewrite *The Waste Land*. The canon's reach
casts ruinous light. The masters' pens breach
this page where my own hand spectates. Babylon
risen, exorcism in reverse, whose nature upended now?
If I remember my own name, then I can ego
my way through this crowd of shadows
that cross the bridge of my back mid-bow.

I slept in the Fifth House of Modernism,
beneath stars that offered no light—dust
full of fear, my own dead skin encrusting
room corners and my mind in a schism
between image and luck. When I awoke,
the empire rose in me and I was risen
from its dead letters to the letter, chiseled
by my own invisibility, this war between smoke

and reflection, between self versus self conniving
in the longest hall of my fear to remain there.
Many doors scraped open, their alabaster
knobs ghost-turned while voices as convincing
as a mother's slipped out. I looked into one room
and found a window broken into a smile, wind
whistling Confederately through the glass.
Tell me why I grinned and hollered back a tune:

"Away! Away! I wish the masters dead." To be freed
I tried to revise *The Waste Land* but blacker,
where Margaret Garner speaks to Margaret Walker
on a barge crossing the Mississippi River. I see
the aftermath of this meeting, slow
in the river mud fondling the delay.
They will make it across. They will pray.
They will drown beneath what they know:

that the living have undone so many
and the river's dark portion was the color
of a baby's dried blood, the neck wound dolorous
in its grin-shaped curve, another mangled
bridge into history. Who could name the salve
between two women death had undone,
one woman so sure of whom she'd undone:
Garner the master. Garner the slave.

The river unfurls its god tongue
in Nigger Jim's voice. He speaks of rivers
as the river, soul grown deep into a river
carving a country like an infant's throat.
There are many ways to freedom, with a hymn's
lithe blade or a butcher knife. Even now the blood
running through the river runs through my hand,
black as a cock that crows for dawn hilt-to-hide till mum.

Dawn does not know it cannot drown me.
Sunrise gilds all water the same dull pageant
and I am water after all. Sun-rinsed,
my skin coal-hisses, a conquered city, the first flame.
Call me Chicago, call me Lake Michigan.
I, an unnatural mirror for enlightenment,
spit back ash rivaling Pompeii. Relent
to whom? For what? Night will come again.

The stars' epistrophes, their bright punctuations,
insult the dark and puncture night again
with haunting past tense. Emblazoned
with myths and maps of light, imagined
cartographies making use of fire and fear,
night will come again, a cover, beast's blanket
or runaway's winter shawl. A cliché of crows sinks
its hatchlings in a man's maw. He rears

their small nights to maturity. He speaks
in sunsets. This is the end of the world.
Even an ended world needs a mythology.
Like snow, like breath, like rust, like feet,
night will come again and over a sobbing
woman who has found her mother's grave
for the first time and succumbed to elegy.
Her cries bleed over the dirt with a strange insistency.

Away, away, a world drowns beneath this knowledge:
Hurston hidden in the Garden of Heavenly Rest.
Eden's daughter in the dust. White dresses nest
in a magnolia. Their bodiless silhouettes
sit watch as the passing season makes tombs
of the trees. Sweet and fresh, the sudden smell
of burning years passes by. Elegies ride the tail-
winds. Splayed bodies for a sail, the womb-

swell of ghosts pushes ships toward a present
filled with flags and saddles, religions and burned drums.
Do not permit them passage, Lord. Imaginations
can be so open and what steps through, what sprints
from the past, is just another unjust symptom
of drapetomania fondling this fiction's curtains.
Do not permit it passage, Lord. A stain
uninvited, there's no telling what light will do. Some

drunk off the street hollers at passersby the interpretation
of "Juba Dis," but no one understands, the hexed threads
of his iris another river to get lost on. What was said
by the hambone hustler harping on predictions
divined from his palms was that love was not enough,
and what I thought was love was only a gateway
for the dead. Once I had a lover, not gutless
but as much imprisoned in himself as he was afraid of

imprisoning me in his splayed body. He would lie
down with me and tell me all the ghosts who rushed
to him in the dark: an uncle who died hard, whose eyes
were the color of two deep injuries; pale women who touched
and gaped at him; a more demonic form the size
of what could have no size that choked him while,
on the other side, his ex-lover slept. This he told me
after thrusting into my mouth as though building for us

a myth to explain what had happened and would inevitably,
again, happen. "I could draw a picture of it for you,"
he said, and, looking around for tools, set about doing
until I told him no. He shared all his so-called demons:
the undead kin, the blood he kept secret, the semen
he didn't. Three years later, in an obscure text,
he tells me this without telling me, as though my own blood
would respond to clues. "I never came in you," he didn't

say. Nor did I not want him to—to say, to come.
Already in me he was and wasn't and I was ready
to be bound to him by the veins. The slum
alphabet of forgiveness petrified my unsteady hand.
I watched from a phone screen's glow my life's
buttons pop all at once and behind the fabric
unhid a new life, ecstatic, gothic with flies.
Blood-bound, a marriage multiplies the fable.

I splayed my body's opiated rooms. Rank
wind galloped from the cavity, dry as the harmattan.
It must be winter in me. Why rush back
into invisibility? Father, is that you? My harm?

> *My father must have seen such sights—*
> *he was very old when he died—*
> *or heard of them,*
> *or had this danger touch him*

my father was not old when he died
but he looked as the possessed look
his face an apiary a wasp den prying
like a fact from a story's gap I shook

him in my nightmares and all the drugs
spilled from the wasp-size holes
never knowing what drug it was
that took him I made them all his to hold

we counted them and they were twelve
my father the Father who carried the end
of civilization which is the beginning of time
in his nose his lungs his mind
in his veins the wash of second chances
he never shared his demons with me
but he made new demons like new dances
to entertain himself the King the king the king

and danger touched him, sniffed
his crown, deemed it unworthy, inedible,
and ate the flesh instead. Perchance this myth:
a giant struts from the Bible,
one man's monster another man's test.
"Be humble," says the hero, "Lil bitch,"
replies the chorus, and the epic of our lives rests
in a radio's top-ten playlist, in the darkness

there where no one will ever see, in the stereo's
electric heart circuiting a boy's chest. John Henry,
let the man breathe, let the reins of his veins go.
Your spooky love won't do, John Henry.
Your boogie-woogie love won't do, a lover's face
carved into a map and who could leave this violet
city—sorry, I meant violent; I meant to trace
the scar on an enslaved woman's forehead

caused by a mule's kick. The scar is the gate.
I think we'll find our answers there, the how
we got here, into the mind of York shaking
a deer off his back for his master to devour.
Into the mind of a darky specimen tamed
by a hug, by a white woman's smile.
Into the mind of a polyester suit framed
by black hands and a white mind. John Henry, chile,

is that you in danger of being touched?
Are you Mapplethorpe's "Super Nigger,"
your hammer near-hand, cool desire cutting
you off from the neck up? Is that you, Bigger?
Should've saw you coming a mile away,
cutting off that white woman's head
'cause you lost your own. Which way
hea'ben be is where I be headin'.

I saw you, Mother Mary, floating in a puddle,
your porcelain neck broken and letting all
the water in. Can't drown that way, cuddled
by the waves you birthed, water your gall
and ointment, your rage and your mercy.
I told a friend to stop messing with the loa
and he heard "the Lord." Have mercy,
my Chicago southern tongue don't know

a from r. Don't know London
from Brooklyn. All bridges lead one place.
Crossing the water, the dead who have undone
so many raise their hands through the surface,
raise their heads in canon. In the wake
of disaster, a wake. In water whelmed with attendance
and attending histories anchored to stakes
anchored to chains clanging panegyrics, another chance.

Heaven is where I'll be headed:
a deer walks to Lake Michigan and sips
from putrid water then looks up, the tips
of its antlers prick the sky like stars lending
soft fire to the scene; a hunter lends his arrow
to its bow and flexes a shoulder blade, elbow bent
to aim into the deer's side a pierced distance.
Air divides from itself to reveal its spectral marrow.

O, choosy god, choose me. The blue-
amber sky requiems my solstice.
I am the longest day of myself, blissed
here in truncated perfection, a hue
of indictments I made into keys.
Shoot me, hunter. By all things planetary,
sweet, I swear the arrowhead's pathway
into me will be the doorway, entry

into my own self-raised heaven. My head
I raze. My Babel tongue a tender memorial.
Glossolalia in exorcism, a territorial
narrative—this glossary of organs, this shedding
of seconds for a pen. I move without editor.
You see this: the blinding light reprimanded,
revision inconclusive, cannons wasting the land, and
the masters, their remnants, garnered in their human error.

IN THE BEGINNING

six children jump Double Dutch in autumn
rain, and the ropes' helix is a seventh seeing.
It opens and closes like an eye-
lid and through its quick-fire lens the smallest
child jumps. Rain in their hair, their bare feet
slap concrete church-rhythmic
as tambourines. I watch the child keep time,
then look past them to the other side
of the rope twirl's wet eye, brick tenements
cementing my seeing to an ancient memory
this game turned gate-into-history creates.
Was it the Door of No Return beckoning *return*,
or the doorway to my grandmother's mind,
her stroke-stunned body stripped of words
yet heavy with language: blink and cry, her hand
tight around my hand, the hospice dizzy
with slow minutes? Her moans cradled both
curse and confession. And those children,
the Beneficent's right hand, sing with the words
my grandmother lost, a rhyme to heal
the days in the whoosh-clack of their twin whip
turned so fast it whistled, their feet escaping
in place. Mercy. Even the gods run
home in stillness, tossing up a spiritual
to greet the falling rain: *Down by the river* /
down by the sea / *you came to find your Savior* /
but instead you found me waiting for
the song to end, the shrill voices
ringing like biloko bells to trap me there
in the ropes' wet pupil shown through to the end
of knowledge where there is no slack, where language
breaks into molecule and memory, skin as percussion,
the glint of diamond in a dope boy's grill, my own
tongue fit for Babel, a fool's end, an end
to one million sins in a single night, the end

of confession of silk of need the day's end
ending at the ropes' ends. End of breath of sound.
Words drop like seeds to this hard, wet ground.

NOTES

"Final Poem as Request for Maskot [. . .]"—"They sure do love them some Black pain" is quoted from Morgan Parker critiquing this peculiar hunger of white editors. For Al Jolson.

"Order of Events"—"Uneasy lies the head that wears a crown" is from William Shakespeare's *King Henry IV, Part 2*. The "Shadows" referenced in the poem are the AAI RQ-7 Shadow, an unmanned drone used for reconnaissance by the U.S., Australian, Swedish, and Italian militaries.

"Tabula Rasa"—The shirt in reference is a reconceptualization of the shirts created by Randi Gloss for GLOSSRAGS, where the names of those recently killed by police are printed in bold white letters on a black shirt so that we will always remember their names.

"Interlude: Sasa and Zamani," as best as I can describe, uses the two ontological dimensions sasa and zamani (Kiswahili) as a way to imagine my father's death as the eventual passage into a *forever* completely distant from my ability to fully grasp. Sasa is the dimension of the immediate past, the present, and the very near future that allows for a dead person to remain "living dead" as long as someone alive remembers them; and zamani shares space with sasa within the immediate past but covers backward from sasa into an infinite wellspring of everything that ever was, a frozen time of myth and history. John Mbiti describes zamani as "the final store-house for all phenomena and events, the ocean of time in which everything becomes absorbed into a reality that is neither after nor before." Someone dead moves into zamani when there is no one alive who remembers them, when all who would have remembered them have themselves traversed into sasa, which is always spilling backward into zamani. For a more in-depth description, please refer to John Mbiti's *African Religions and Philosophy* (1970) and La Vinia Delois Jennings's *Toni Morrison and the Idea of Africa* (2008).

"Final Poem for Amiri Baraka"—The character Crow Jane appears in a series of poems by Amiri Baraka. In "An Interview with Amiri Baraka," conducted by William J. Harris (*Conversations with Amiri Baraka*, ed. Charlie Reilly, 1994), Baraka says, "[S]he has got to be killed off because there is no further use—I can't get anything else from her. Crow Jane is the white Muse appropriated by the black experience." The "three-toed frog" is mentioned in Nina Simone's striking song "Dambala," from her album *It Is Finished* (RCA Records, 1974). Damballah is a loa/lwa in Haitian Vodou and is commonly known as the Sky Father.

"The Flying African"—This poem is based on the folktale of the flying African who taught enslaved Africans how to fly back to Africa. The story is often considered a retelling of the historical event of Igbo Landing, where Igbo captives who were purchased in Savannah, Georgia, were then boarded on a small ship heading to St. Simons Island. On board, the enslaved Igbos revolted, drowning their captors and grounding the vessel at a nearby marshland. It is at this marshland where they chose mass suicide by walking into the water, singing, "The Water Spirit brought us. The Water Spirit will take us home," a reference to their supreme being, Chukwu. This location is known as Igbo Landing. Amadioha is an alusi (spirit) of the storm for the Igbo people.

"Final Poem for the 'Black Body'" uses an edited image of the slave ship *Brookes* from "Description of a Slave Ship" (1789, woodcut) at the British Museum.

"Final Poem as Tidalectic Elegy" takes its quotes, in order of appearance, from: "'The Water Is Waiting': Water Tidalectics, and Materiality" by T. Mars McDougall (*Liquid Blackness*, volume 3, issue 6), "Ocean" by Alice Smith (*She*, Rainwater Recordings, 2013), *In the Wake* by Christina Sharpe (Duke University Press, 2016). The italics *"sunken Africans will give AIDS to the sharks"* is a comment someone left on a YouTube video I watched years ago that depicted a small barge of many African migrants begging for help while being ignored by sailors on a ship, one of whom recorded that very video. The ending to section two hearkens back to Ellen Bryant Voigt's poem "Largesse" from her book *Shadow of Heaven* (Norton, 2003). "Church's" refers to the restaurant Church's Chicken.

"January 28, 1918"—Porvenir was a small West Texas border town. The Texas Rangers of Company B (led by Captain James Monroe Fox), the Eighth U.S. Cavalry Regiment, and four Anglo-American ranchers killed fifteen men and boys there. This poem uses the NBC News article "Porvenir,

Texas' Details Massacre of Mexican Americans by U.S. Soldiers, Rangers" by Raul A. Reyes (September 27, 2019), and "Remembering the Porvenir Massacre" by Justin Minsker from the Texas Historical Commission (January 25, 2019).

"'Ne Me Quitte Pas': *I Put a Spell on You*: Nina Simone: 1965" is inspired by Frank Bidart and Eduardo Corral. This poem is my interpretation of the art genre "Whose sleeves?" The French is from Belgian singer-songwriter Jacques Brel's "Ne Me Quitte Pas" (1959).

"Final Poem for the Moon" is inspired by and for Natalie Diaz.

"Final Poem for Grandma Elizabeth's Cancer" is an acrostic.

"Mastery" is a poem that references many artworks, songs, spiritualities, literary works, and folktales. Due to the loss of my office from water damage post-fire, I lost the notebook that contained most of these allusions and nods. To the best of my ability, I will list what immediately comes to mind with deep apologies for any information I leave out:

1. *The Waste Land* by T. S. Eliot is referenced throughout the poem.
2. "Dixie" (1859), composed by Daniel Decatur Emmett
3. *Beloved* by Toni Morrison
4. *The Adventures of Tom Sawyer* by Mark Twain
5. "The Negro Speaks of Rivers" by Langston Hughes
6. "Her cries bleed over the dirt with a strange insistency." —Margaret Walker
7. "Garden of Heavenly Rest" is where Zora Neale Hurston is buried.
8. "Eden's daughter in the dust" is a nod to Julie Dash.
9. "Sweet and fresh, the sudden smell"—"Strange Fruit" (1937), composed by Abel Meeropol
10. "drapetomania"—A "disease" meant to explain why enslaved Africans ran away from slavery. See Samuel A. Cartwright for more details.
11. "Juba Dis" is from the rhyme "Juba Juba," meant to accompany the dance pattin' juba, aka hambone. The dance originated from enslaved Kongo peoples and consists of stomping, clapping, and patting the arms, thighs, hips, face, chest, and shoulders in intricate rhythms,

mimicking drums when drums were made illegal for fear of their ability to facilitate slave revolts.

12. The entire stanza beginning with "My father must have seen such sights" is quoted from James Baldwin's essay "Nobody Knows My Name."

13. The phrase *"the King the king* the king" is a nod to Carl Phillips's poem "The King of Hearts," from his book *Cortège*.

14. "Be humble," "Lil bitch"—"Humble" by Kendrick Lamar (2017)

15. "John Henry" speaks to the folktale of John Henry and the mental health issue known as "John Henryism" in the Black community.

16. *Jazz* by Toni Morrison

17. *The Known World* by Edward P. Jones

18. "York" is the enslaved African who ostensibly led the Lewis and Clark Expedition.

19. "Man in Polyester Suit" (1980)—photograph by Robert Mapplethorpe

20. *Uncle Tom's Cabin* by Harriet Beecher Stowe

21. For Mapplethorpe's commentary of "super nigger," see page 83 of *Women's Bodies*, edited by Jane Arthurs and Jean Grimshaw, A&C Black, 1999.

22. *Native Son* by Richard Wright

23. "Mother Mary," or Our Lady of Conception, is the saint syncretized to the orisha Yemanjá of Candomblé spiritual practice in Brazil.

24. The image of the hunter hunting a deer and the sentence "O, choosy god, choose me" allude to the orisha Ọ̀ṣọ́ọ̀sì (Ifá)/Oshosi (Santería)/ Oxóssi (Candomblé).

25. "By all things planetary, sweet" —Gwendolyn Brooks

"In the Beginning"—The grandmother in this poem is my paternal grandmother, Mattie Ford, whom I love and miss. The eloko, plural biloko [Mongo-Nkundo language], is a dwarflike creature of Zaire that hypnotizes its victims with bells to more easily devour them. They are thought to be ancestors of the people who lived in the forests and are considered vicious to and begrudging of the living.

ACKNOWLEDGMENTS

Poems appearing in *Mutiny* have appeared, sometimes as different versions, in the following publications:

American Poetry Review—"The Void"

Bennington Review—"Final Poem for the White Students Next Door Who say 'Nigga' When Singing Along to Rap Songs Loud Enough for Me to Hear" as "Maskot #3: For the White Students Next Door Who say 'Nigga' When Singing Along to Rap Songs Loud Enough for Me to Hear"

Boston Review— "Final First Poem"; "Final Poem as Request for Maskot for White-ran Journal, or 'They sure do love them some black pain.'" as "Maskot #1: They sure do love them some Black pain"; and "Final Poem for Persona" as an excerpt from the poem "The River"

Brick—"Final Poem for the Biography of a Black Man as Animal and His Enforced Embrace of a Human Praxis"

Connotations Press—"Judgment" as "Wild is the Wind"

The Enchanting Verses Literary Review—"The Asphodel"

Kenyon Review—"Final Poem for the Moon"

The Missouri Review—"Tabula Rasa" and "The Field"

The Nation—"Final Poem for the 'Field of Poetry'"

The New Yorker—"Final Poem for My Father Misnamed in My Mouth"

The Paris Review—"Mastery" and "'Ne Me Quitte Pas:' I Put a Spell on You: Nina Simone: 1965"

Poem-a-day at Poetry.org—"And Now Upon My Head the Crown," "Hunter," and "Order of Events"

The Poetry Review—"The Flying African" and "Herald"

Primal School—"Of the Question of Self and How It Never Quite Gets Answered"

Sewanee Review—"Final Poem for Amiri Baraka" and "Final Poem for the Famous Poet"

The Shade Journal—"Final Poem for War During War" as "excerpt from 'Interruptive'"

Southern Indiana Review—"Final Poem for the Bullet"

TriQuarterly—"Final Poem for the Deer," "In the Beginning . . ."

The Yale Review—"Mushmouf's Maybe Crown"

"Final Poem for My Grandma Elizabeth's Cancer" appeared in the chapbook *Burn* (YesYes Books 2012).

"Mastery" was translated into French by Pierre Vinclair for the journal *Catastrophes*.

I would like to thank the following people for their unconditional support and presence, with the hope of being forgiven for anyone I forget:

Joel Dias-Porter, Saddiq Dzukogi, Aricka Foreman, Hafizah Geter, Rebecca Gayle Howell, Luther Hughes, Ashaki Jackson, Taylor Johnson, Bettina Judd, Donika Kelly, Willie Kinard III, Shayla Lawson, Nabila Lovelace, Airea D. Matthews, Ron G. Mitchell, Cheswayo Mphanza, Nicholas Nichols, Nkosi Nkululeko, Khadijah Queen, Erika Sanchez, Safiya Sinclair, Jayson Smith, and Marcus Wicker.

Special thanks to Keith S. Wilson for helping me with "Final Poem for the 'Black Body.'" You're a genius.

To my editors, Paul Slovak and Allie Merola, you are amazing. To everyone at Penguin/Viking, thank you so much for your hard work on this book.

Huge thank-you to my agent, Bill Clegg, and everyone at the Clegg Agency, especially Simon Toop.

The Harvard Radcliffe Institute, National Endowment for the Arts, and the Whiting Foundation for time and support. To my friends and colleagues at Bennington College and Randolph low-res MFA for collegiality and camaraderie.

Beowulf Sheehan

Phillip B. Williams is from Chicago, Illinois, and is the author of the book *Thief in the Interior* (Alice James, 2016). A recipient of the Kate Tufts Discovery Award, Lambda Literary Award, and Whiting Award, he has also received fellowships from the Radcliffe Institute for Advanced Study at Harvard University and the National Endowment for the Arts. He currently teaches at Bennington College and the Randolph College low-residency MFA.

PENGUIN POETS

PENGUIN POETS